What people are sa

The Sacred Gathas of Zarathushtra & the Old Avestan Canon

Beneficial to those who want to understand the primary message of Zarathushtra as recited in the Gathas!
Homi D. Gandhi, Former President of FEZANA (Federation of Zoroastrian Associations of North America) and Current Co-Chair of the FEZANA Interfaith Activities Committee

The Gathas of Zarathushtra, as translated by Pablo Vazquez, are very easy to follow and understand. The Avestan approach in translation is highly commendable. I would highly recommend this book.
Mobed Kerman Katrak, Zoroastrian priest, North American Mobeds Council

It is way past time that our religion, history, and culture is told through a lens that reflects our community and our people. Pablo Vazquez's translation corrects decades of false reliance on underinformed and biased translations made by Eurocentric translators that didn't care to deliver the deeper meaning of Gathas through their translation. This book will help us, and our next generations, fully capture the deep meanings of the Gathas in ways that were never before captured.
Parshan Khosravi, Co-Chair of the Zoroastrian Youth of North America and Chair of the 7th World Zoroastrian Youth Congress

A critical resource for students and scholars of Zoroastrian tradition. Faithful and beautiful, rigorous while remaining accessible. A profound achievement and contribution to the field.

Dr. Michael Muhammad Knight, Religious Studies Scholar and Author of *Muhammad's Body: Baraka Networks and the Prophetic Assemblage*

Pablo Vazquez, though a convert to Zoroastrianism, is a true lover of Zarathushtra. His is a fresh and revolutionary voice necessary in the faith and the world over. His translation of the Gathas, the only hymns of Zarathushtra we have, are important because they make clear that these core texts of Zoroastrianism reject the precepts of bigotry and intolerance found in some later Sassanian texts. As a queer Zoroastrian, I wish nothing but success for this book and call for all Zoroastrians to welcome the LGBTQ+ community to which the translator and I belong.

Hoshang Merchant, modern India's first openly gay major poet and author of *Yaraana: Gay Writing from South Asia*

This is an accessible version of the Gathas written by the author for "modern audiences." The author's passion for Zoroastrianism and knowledge of it is clearly evident from the very first pages. A great addition to any collection on the topic.

Payam Nabarz, author of *The Mysteries of Mithras* and editor of *Anahita: Ancient Persian Goddess and Zoroastrian Yazata*

The Sacred Gathas of Zarathushtra & the Old Avestan Canon

A Modern Translation of
Ancient Wisdom

The Sacred Gathas of Zarathushtra & the Old Avestan Canon

A Modern Translation of
Ancient Wisdom

Pablo Vazquez

MANTRA
BOOKS

Winchester, UK
Washington, USA

JOHN HUNT PUBLISHING

First published by Mantra Books, 2022
Mantra Books is an imprint of John Hunt Publishing Ltd., No. 3 East Street, Alresford
Hampshire SO24 9EE, UK
office@jhpbooks.com
www.johnhuntpublishing.com
www.mantra-books.net

For distributor details and how to order please visit the 'Ordering' section on our website.

ISBN: 978 1 78535 961 3
978 1 78535 962 0 (ebook)
Library of Congress Control Number: 2021941981

A CIP catalogue record for this book is available from the British Library.

Design: Matthew Greenfield

UK: Printed and bound by CPI Group (UK) Ltd, Croydon, CR0 4YY
Printed in North America by CPI GPS partners

We operate a distinctive and ethical publishing philosophy in
all areas of our business, from our global network of authors to
production and worldwide distribution.

Contents

Preface

What you are about to read is the core and central text for one of the oldest, most complex, and heavily influential spiritual traditions in history. Mazdayasna, known popularly in the English-speaking world as Zoroastrianism, was once the world's largest religion with its influence stretching from China to Egypt but now, as of the time of this writing, it could very well number less than 150,000 in declared adherents. With a theology and cosmology that continuously adapts and evolves to its historical-geographic circumstances without sacrificing its essence, it is also exceedingly versatile which has allowed it to survive all sorts of calamities and massive changes during its more than 3000-year history. The Gathas, the poems of Zarathushtra, and the surrounding Old Avestan canon, are some of the oldest spiritual texts still extant to us and they remain the main unchanging core of Mazdayasna which all adherents, no matter their theological and philosophical orientations, hold in common as dear and sacred.

This translation is my gift back to Mazdayasna as it is the source of not just my journey towards the Path of Asha but also the very core of my ethics. This book is not a declaration of my theological outlook but merely an attempt to provide the best and most accessible translation I could provide for the modern seeker. The reader can read more about my translation process in the Translation Notes section of the book but note here as I repeat elsewhere that this work was a combination of academic rigor, poetic display, and, most importantly to me, devotional action. It is my deepest desire that you gain as much wisdom from the Gathas as so many have before in history. I definitely have and in these times of chaos and turmoil these texts bring a new clarity to our realities.

All thanks, worship, adoration, and praise are due to Ahura

Mazda, the source of all, to the glorious Ashavan Zarathushtra, and to the Yazata and the Fravashis of the Ashavans past, present, and future, and to my honored ancestors. Many grateful thanks to the professors, former and current, at the Shapoorji Pallonji Institute of Zoroastrian Studies at SOAS University of London who have enriched my academic knowledge of Mazdayasna especially my dear supervisor Dr. Sarah Stewart. Your work towards the academic preservation and study of Mazdayasni knowledge makes you all Ashavans and treasures of our community.

I also declare blessings upon blessings upon my Mazdayasni community from those who have welcomed to those who have not, and especially to my fellow converts who strive to learn and worship as Mazdayasnis. My praise to Mobed Behram Deboo, who conducted my Navjote/Sedreh Pooshi, and to my dear and wonderful Mazdayasni friends who have become so many that to list them here would need a section of its own. Your warmth and welcome of me will never be forgotten and know I treasure our friendships fully. Last, but not least, love and gratefulness to my family, my partners, and my non-Mazdayasni friends and colleagues who have been blessings to me throughout my work and life.

Ushta te (joy be upon you) and may the words of Zarathushtra enlighten you.

P.V.

2021

Foreword

The thing that has always inspired me most about the teachings of Zarathushtra is his exhortation for us to take part in a cosmic struggle against the forces of darkness. For Zarathushtra, it is a struggle between two forces, Asha and Druj, truth and falsehood. One leads towards fullness, wholeness, eternity, power, and love; the other to pain, oppression, suffering and death. Zarathushtra's teachings have certainly directly impacted on all our lives through the revolutionary ideas of the Gathas that have significantly influenced, both directly and indirectly, Christianity, Judaism, Islam, Buddhism, Baha'iism, Greek philosophy, and more. Indeed, they have been the moral compass of Western civilization and beyond.

However, the idea I find most empowering is that it is every man and woman's free will what to do, their responsibility as to which path to take. It is we human beings who, by choosing truth and justice, every day, over and over, bring about the victory of Asha.

The teachings of my prophet Zarathushtra have been the inspiration behind my drive towards public service, fighting injustice, and founding the ASHA Centre in the Royal Forest of Dean, Britain. My aim has been to help people all over the world, especially the young, to navigate the challenges of our contemporary and unpredictable world. The ASHA Centre is a place where people connect with each other in joyful community, immerse themselves in the inspirational beauty of nature, and address profound issues of personal development and the betterment of society. In other words, to choose to live magnificent lives. The idea of human agency is embedded in the "frame-story" of the Gathas, Zarathushtra's own words. That story tells of how the "Soul of the Cow" appeals to the Creator for a protector...

For the ancient Indo-Iranians, the "Soul of the Cow" was a

symbol of Mother Nature, a beautiful image of the earth as gentle, feminine, and nourishing, but here, as now, in need of protection against the forces of pillage and wrath. What I find especially fascinating is that this story is also found within Indian literature, in the Sanskrit Epics and Puranas. The tale therefore must have been an especially ancient one, an "Indo-Iranian" story, told before the one people split into two nations. However, there is a difference in the later Indian versions of the story, and it is revealing. In the Indian versions (probably written at least a thousand years or so after Zarathushtra's), the Cow's appeal results in the Great God himself, Vishnu, descending to earth in human form, as the Avatars Rama or Krishna. In the (more ancient) Iranian version in the Gathas, it is not the Creator, Ahura Mazda, who deals with the problem directly, but instead a man, "a weak poet," Zarathushtra, who is sent.

This is where the difference gets especially interesting because in the Zoroastrian version, the Cow then complains! Asha itself must intervene to justify the sending of a mere man. This suggests, I think, that the Zoroastrian version of the story, even though it's much older, was the more unusual and innovative version of the ancient myth story: why else would there be a need for justification? The Indian version just finishes with the descent of Vishnu, an uncontroversial act by the God in comparison to the sending of Zarathushtra! But what does this difference mean? I think it shows that the poet of the Gathas wanted to emphasize the importance of human agency. For him divine grace – salvation of the world – would come through human beings freely choosing to act for the good and, for the people of ancient Iran and India, this was a new idea.

The older I have become, the more depth I have found in Zarathushtra's pioneering and empowering idea of free will. He does not prescribe what is and is not to be done in demanding terms. Rather, for him, it is the consciousness behind the deed that matters: in Zarathushtra's language, Vohu Manah, the "Right

Mentality." I like that. It seems flexible and subtle, appropriate to the complexities of life and the human mind. The Gathas, although one of the most ancient sacred texts in the world, are an inspiration to us for how to live a good life today. It awes me how, across the millennia, so much of it speaks to us now with such peculiar relevance and immediacy. It is as though modern concerns were implicitly understood and advocated for by the radical poet-seer of the Ancient Iranian peoples. He seems to touch on freedom of thought, female autonomy, the plight of the vulnerable, social justice, animal welfare, sustainable living, and even inclusive spirituality. How wonderful to think a document so ancient can also be so progressive!

For example, the Yatha Ahu Vairyo manthra speaks of Ahura Mazda's support for the poor:

> Worthy and chosen through Asha are they, the Ratus throughout the world, who bring enlightenment to the world, through deeds done on behalf of Ahura Mazda, who has become the advocate of the impoverished. (Y. 27:13)

Another example, on the importance of free will and making the right choices in life:

> When these two spirits come to a confrontation, one must decide on that eternal question: To choose life and growth or the opposite? With this, one must decide on how they will align until the end: Will they choose to align to Druj and deceit, in the worst of all existences, or will they be Ashavans for whom enlightenment awaits? (Y. 30.4)

On the importance of resisting injustice, for me a key catalyst in my fight against all forms of slavery and discrimination, the Gathas say:

May none of those truly devoted to the ways of Druj reach us with manthras and teachings. They will use their delusions to bring our houses, towns, provinces, and the nations of the land in a ruinous state. The recourse for them is our resistance. (Y. 31.18)

The Gathas also have a universal spirit, encouraging us to seek wisdom wherever it exists, meaning wisdom is not limited to the Gathas. How generous and wise!

We thus desire to be those who will bring magnificence to what exists, Oh Mazda and you other Ahuras, alongside the renovators and Asha, when we have centered our thoughts wherever wisdom and understanding may be found. (Y. 30.9)

The Gathas of Zarathushtra, extraordinarily, offer us a glimpse into the heart and mind of a Bronze Age Seer. In words of unsurpassed beauty and sophistication, the ancient Iranian poet depicts his passionate relationship with his God. This foremost Divinity, the "Wise Lord," the poet sees as the creator of virtue, purity, wholeness, eternity, power, and love. The poet's words touch on his own life and struggles, his relationships, and ideals. Above all, they depict his revolutionary understanding of God and of humanity's relationship to a higher spiritual order of reality. As a literary document of such antiquity, bridging the personal and the mystical, they are entirely unique.

I recommend all those who seek enlightenment to read this new publication of the Gathas, in all its poetic beauty, translated by a devoted, young scholar of Zoroastrianism, Pablo Vazquez, who was transformed by the Gathas and became a Zoroastrian through its words. It will leave them inspired to become living Ashavans in their fight against the forces of darkness in the many forms they confront us today.

Zerbanoo Gifford

Author, Former Director of Anti-Slavery International and Charities Aid Foundation India, Award-Winning Human Rights Campaigner, Founder of the ASHA Centre, and a Knight of the Honourable Society of the Knights of the Round Table

Translator's Notes

When translating and compiling this collection of the Old Avestan canon that includes the Gathas, Yasna Haptanghaiti, and the most sacred manthras of Mazdayasna, I took an approach which is sorely lacking in all Avestan translations. Most translations either take massive poetic liberties to align the text to certain movements and/or theological and philosophical schools, thus obscuring their original meanings, or are starkly literal and academic and thus lose all their poetry and spirituality. It must be noted that Avestan was originally a completely oral language and was written down long after the composition of the Avesta. My approach was to both painstakingly translate the Avestan text literally and listen to the liturgical recitations so that moments of emphasis and other poetic inflections would be considered. My translation is primarily not a fully academic work but rather a work of true devotion that takes the literal meanings and gives them the poetic and spiritual quality and essence they deserve. I have restructured many verses grammatically from Avestan and used simpler synonyms than most translations to make the texts readable to a modern audience while maintaining their spiritual core, lessons, and poetry.

I thought it wise to keep over 15 different translations of these texts from differing sources and times open and ready for reference because it is foolish to think that a translation of the Old Avestan canon is just the work of any singular person. Avestan is notoriously difficult to understand, and I fear that, without the discovery of an "Avestan Rosetta Stone," all Avestan translations are, at best, educated speculation. My use/study of these translations acted to further increase my knowledge and understanding of this ancient and liturgical language, particularly during difficulties in choosing proper wording. Readers will notice there is an "Avestan Glossary" included to explain that which I feel should not be translated as there are terms, especially those used as proper nouns in surrounding texts and those whose provenances are mysterious, that have many meanings and interpretations per word and therefore translating them would be declaring a bias and doing a severe disservice to the text. I leave it up to the reader, with the aid of the Glossary, to interpret these terms as they are enlightened to through Asha.

I sought out translation notes and other writings from previous translators and related scholars to learn why certain terminologies were used and quickly realized that most European and American translators from the 1800s and early 1900s oriented Mazdayasni texts towards an Abrahamic (and particularly Protestant) paradigm filtered through an orientalist lens. Endeavoring to avoid this, endemic as it is when non-adherents translate sacred texts, I studied the philosophies, linguistics, and cultural perceptions of historical Mazdayasna (especially Pre-Islamic and Pahlavi Mazdayasna) alongside the cultures and peoples that had either a large Mazdayasna presence or a developed historical relationship with Mazdayasna. I have avoided using terms like "good" or "evil" and have introduced terms like "virtuous" and "enlightened" which fit the historical and cultural contexts of these texts. This avoids a cultural bias towards Abrahamic theological/cultural thinking as there is much baggage attached even to such simple terminology. I have also chosen to use Mazdayasna instead of Zoroastrianism in this text so that natively-used terminology and the proper name of the tradition is used more and gets public exposure.

Considering this is primarily a translation of the Old Avestan canon, it constitutes most of this book, but some of the Young Avestan verses, which surround and praise the texts, are also included. The Gathas and Yasna Haptanghaiti are not dry intellectual exercises and should not be consistently interrogated for scholarly purity. These are the core and most ancient texts of Mazdayasna, and I felt it important to include such Young Avestan verses which are presented in Italics to differentiate them from the Old Avestan canon and to prevent confusion. Some verses include a numbered parenthetical multiplier denoting how many times they were recited during the reading and adoration of the texts to aid the readers in their spiritual engagement.

My hope with these translations, the raison d'être of this project, was to make these texts fully accessible to the modern reading public and to provide a clearer and unbiased presentation of the beautiful messages, stories, wisdom, and poetry provided therein. I do this out of love for Ahura Mazda, the Amesha Spenta, and the Yazata, and for the spread of spiritual teachings of Mazdayasna to all conscious beings in this material realm. May we all be blessed and empowered through Asha now and forever.

Avestan Glossary

Ahura Mazda: The highest divinity in Mazdayasna, the source of Asha, and of all spiritual and material existence. Ahura is thought to mean "lord"/"sovereign"/"master" and is used plurally referencing other divinities. Ahuric is used as an appellation applied to certain terms and concepts to denote them as being of the highest value and merit. Mazda is thought to mean "wisdom"/"wise"/ "knowledgeable" and though used sometimes separately to Ahura it is always referential as the name of this divinity. Ahura Mazda is popularly translated as "Wise Lord" and the spiritual teachings of Ahura Mazda are labeled Mazdayasna, "the worship/veneration/exaltation [-yasna, also the name of the main liturgical Avestan text in which the Gathas traditionally reside] of the Wise One/wisdom/ knowledge [Mazda-]."

Asha: The spiritual force that permeates all, sourced from Ahura Mazda, and embodied in the Amesha Spenta Asha Vahishta (see below) as noted in the texts. Asha is thought to mean "truth"/"cosmic order"/"righteousness"/"spiritual power." The texts promote alignment to Asha and the Path of Asha through engagement in virtuous thought, word, and deed along with requested worship and praise. A master of Asha is an Ashavan and something full of Asha is called Ashavic.

Amesha Spenta: A category of beings that directly share the same essence and nature as Ahura Mazda, noted as "being of him" and represented in the texts as both these beings and their embodied concepts. The texts exhort the readers and listeners to embody these concepts and provide worship to the beings as they are direct manifestations of Ahura Mazda. Amesha is thought to mean "immortals"/"divinities" and Spenta "bountiful"/"blessed"/"providential"/"holy." These Amesha Spenta, of which seven are named in the text, are: Ameretat ("immortality"/

11

"perpetuity"/"continuance"), Armaiti ("devotion"/"harmony"), Asha Vahishta (see "Asha" above, Vahishta is thought to mean "best"/"greatest"/"most honored"), Haurvatat ("wholeness"/ "perfection"/"completion"/"holistic nature"), Spenta Mainyu (see aforementioned "Spenta," Mainyu is thought to mean "sp irit"/"mentality"/"consciousness"), Vohu Manah ("virtuous mind"/"virtuous thought"/"virtuous purpose"/"blessed intellect"), and Xshatra ("authority"/"power"/"command"/"do minion").

Yazata: The category of divinities after the Amesha Spenta whose title is thought to mean "those worthy of worship/ veneration." Like the Amesha Spenta, they represent both unique beings and embodied concepts and are of the same essence but not completely of the same nature as Ahura Mazda, who stands far beyond them, and the Amesha Spenta, who are in complete unity with Ahura Mazda. Those named in the texts are Airyaman (patron and healer of the community; "fellows hip"/"community"/"brethrenship"), the Apas (patrons of the waters; "waters"/"streams"), Ashi (patron of divine rewards and blessings; "rewards"/"gifts"/"blessings"/"riches"), Atar (patron of the holy fire; "fire"/"flames"/etc.), Hvare (patron of the Sun; "Sun"/"solar"/"star"), Mithra (patron of promises and covenants; "covenant"/"alliance"/"promise"), Sraosha (patron of one's conscience; "conscience"/"observance"/"obedience"), Vata-Vayu (patron of the wind and atmosphere with both names used interchangeably and separately; "wind"/"gusts" [vayu] and "atmosphere"/"aether" [vata], Verethragna [patron of victory and overcoming defeat; "smiter of obstacles"/"victorious over obstacles"), Xvarenah (patron of divine glory and divine mystic power; "glory"/"splendor"/"anointment"), and Zam (patron of the Earth; "Earth" "land"/"soil").

The Spitama Clan: Members of Zarathushtra's family of which little is known through the texts aside that they endorse his spiritual teachings. As these are markedly proper names, no translation will be provided. The Spitamids mentioned in the texts are Haecataspa, Maidyoimaongha, Pourucista, and Zarathushtra.

Other Personalities: These are figures who are not Spitamids and are either as allies or enemies of Zarathushtra and his spiritual teachings. Some are historical figures referenced by Zarathushtra to illustrate a point. Allies include Frashaoshtra Hvogva (follower of Zarathushtra), Jamaspa Hvogva (follower of Zarathushtra), and Vishtaspa (patron of Zarathushtra). Enemies include Bendva (tyrannical chieftain) and Graehma (corrupt rival priest). Historical figures mentioned, bereft of context in the texts, are Friya (parent of Tura), Tura (honored person), Vivahvan (parent of Yima), and Yima (criminal against cattle and people).

Titles: Titles used in the texts for myriad people in myriad ways. These are Karapan (a class of priests), Kavi (a class of nobles), Manthran (ritual performers of the Manthras, a term thought to mean "sacred formulas"/"holy songs"/"blessed prayers"), Ratu (a position thought to mean "learned master"/"judge"/"decision-provider"), Saoshyants (a category used for the community of believers as a whole thought to mean "those who bring benefit/charity/renovation"), Usij (another class of priests), Zaotar (an honored position thought to mean "chief priest"/"master invoker"/"officiating cleric").

Druj: The completely opposite and opposing force to Asha which is of a weaker nature and essence but is nonetheless viewed as an annoyance and/or threat. Druj is thought to mean "the lie"/"the deception"/"dishonesty"/"corruption." A Drujvan is a master of Druj.

Daeva: Beings of a lower spiritual nature worshipped by Zarathushtra's rivals and viewed as unambiguously unvirtuous and born from unvirtuous thought. Daeva is thought to mean "those to be rejected"/"the cast aside ones." The only Daeva mentioned by name in the texts is Aeshma, the patron of wrath thought to mean "wrath"/"rage"/"violent malice."

Other Terms: Chinvat Bridge (metaphorical and/ or metaphysical location thought to mean "bridge of choice"/"path of decision"/"narrow crossing"), Gatha ("poems"/"songs"/"hymns"), Haptanghaiti ("seven chapters/ sections/stanzas"), and Tushna Matai (words of unknown provenance believed to be, in latter Mazdayasna, either a form of meditation, trance ritual, or a method of communicating/ traveling with/in the spiritual realm).

The Holy Manthras: Yatha Ahu Vairyo, Ashem Vohu, and Yenghe Hatam

Yasna 27:13–14

27.13: Worthy and chosen through Asha are they, the Ratus throughout the world, who bring enlightenment to the world, through deeds done on behalf of Ahura Mazda, who has become the advocate of the impoverished. (x4)

27.14: Asha is virtuous and magnificent, and joy upon joy is what Asha provides, for thus is Asha Vahishta. (x3)

27.15: *We worship the Ahuna Vairya, and we worship Asha Vahishta who is the most beautiful of the Amesha Spenta.* They that are, who are of any gender, Ahura Mazda knows through Asha of their glorious sacrifices: Thus, we offer them worship!

The Ahunavaiti Gatha

Yasna 28

28.0: *We plead now for the thought, we plead now for the word, we plead now for the deed, all of which are of Ashavan Zarathushtra. May the Amesha Spenta welcome the Gathas. Oh Ashavic Gathas, all reverence is due to you.*

28.1: Oh Mazda, I raise my hands out in prayer to glorify the blessings of Asha through which my intellect is enriched, and the spirit of the cow is honored.

28.2: I am here to aid you, Ahura Mazda, through Vohu Manah who unlocks for me the blessings of Asha in the realm of thought and spirit, and the realm of matter, where the faithful are brought comfort.

28.3: Oh Ahura Mazda, whose power never fades, along with Asha, and Vohu Manah, and Armaiti, I ask you all to come to my aid for I will praise you as no one has before.

28.4: So that all may know Ahura Mazda's rewards for their actions, I will guide their spirits towards Asha with both the aid of Vohu Manah and my own ability.

28.5: Oh Asha, is it through Vohu Manah that I may perceive your glory? Ahura Mazda resides in me, through the manthras that drive even the unvirtuous and beastly towards truth, through which Sraosha strengthens me.

28.6: Come to me, Vohu Manah, so that Asha may grant to me, Zarathushtra, and to all believers the eternal blessings of Mazda's glorious teachings and promised aid through which we will overcome the assailments of our enemies.

28.7: Oh Asha, grant the blessings of Vohu Manah! Oh Armaiti, grant vigor to Vishtaspa and to me. Oh Mazda, grant all these blessings and grant us the manthras through which we learn of your glory.

28.8: Oh glorious Ahura, harmonious with glorious Asha, I

ask with love for the eternal blessings of Vohu Manah which were bestowed on the heroic Frashaoshtra not just for me but also for all those throughout time who have earned your blessings.

28.9: Oh Ahura Mazda and Asha, who provide us with a glorious mind and have the power to invigorate and bless us, we hope to banish through our songs of praise the disappointment which you have endured.

28.10: Oh Ahura Mazda, bring prosperity to those you witness as just and worthy, who are aligned with Asha through their virtuous thoughts, for I know prayer is effective and their words will lead to the dispersal of your bounty.

28.11: Oh Ahura Mazda, whose spiritual teachings make manifest the timeless truths of Asha and Vohu Manah, enlighten us with the prayerful words that brought forth the essence of existence.

Yasna 29

29.1: The spirit of the cow, whose wailings you heard, spoke and said: "Who am I made for? Who made me? All I have known is violence and savagery wrought by Aeshma through whom might and rage are tools of oppression. I have never known another herdsman and so you must be the one to bring me the blessed pastures I desire."

29.2: The spirit of the cow, who spoke then to Asha, asked thus: "Is there someone you can bring whose virtuous discernment leads them towards diligent care and feeding of the cow? Who can be its master with the power to cast away violence and those corrupted by Druj?"

29.3: Asha, having heard these words, replied thus: "There is no such helpful being to be found who can cast them away. In all surveyed lands, near and far, the wisdom of acting virtuously towards the disadvantaged has been lost. I will aid the one who calls me, though, for they will be powerful beyond comparison."

29.4: "Mazda is all-knowing and can perceive the reasonings and paths, past and future, of the mortals and even the Daeva. Empowered to decide thereof, what this Ahura wills shall be."

29.5: "Oh Ahura Mazda, we both, my spirit and that of the cow, unite in raising our hands out in prayer so that we may both urge you to hear our supplications. A life full of destruction wrought by those corrupted by Druj is not a life for those who live virtuously or for the caretakers of the animals and fields."

29.6: Ahura Mazda, who is the wise master of the teachings, spoke thus: "I have found no master or Ratu aligned to the Path of Asha which I have set for you and your care under the herdsman and the farmer."

29.7: Ahura Mazda, who is holy and one with Asha, has given the milk and fat of cattle through his ordering to them that seek nourishment. Thus, the spirit of the cow asks: "Vohu Manah, who have you then found to care for us?"

29.8: Vohu Manah thus replied: "I have found Zarathushtra Spitama, who amongst all listens to our teachings, and wants to sing the praises of us all, of you Oh Mazda, and of Asha, so that we may enjoy the beauty of his words."

29.9: Lamenting, the soul of the cow spoke thus: "Am I meant to be content with an impotent and weak poet as my caretaker when I desire a master who, through Xshatra, is strong? When will this desire of mine, of one capable of aiding me, be fulfilled?"

29.10: Oh Ahura, bless us all with strength through the power of Vohu Manah and Asha so that our homes may be virtuous and peaceful. It is you, Oh Mazda, who was the first to provide such blessings even before what is.

29.11: Where else can I find the power of Asha and virtuous thought? Oh soul of the cow, recognize me as the aid promised to you by the one blessed with foresight and vision, which is you, Oh Mazda, who brings me forward as a gift. Oh Ahura, glorious as you are, join us at this moment!

Yasna 30

30.1: I proclaim now, to those who listen, praises for the Ahura and Vohu Manah, who already know of my blessed words and those you shall say for them. Delightful blessings will come through the lights of the holy to those who learn the teachings of Asha.

30.2: Open your ears to these glorious matters! Gaze upon the radiance and center your thoughts on the divine invitations gained through your singular choices, ones that each must make for themselves, before it is announced to us as expected that the moment of our grand communion has come.

30.3: The great choice, by which the charitable ones choose correctly while the miserly do not, is between the twin spirits who have existed since the start of what is, manifesting themselves in our minds and visions, who are opposites in thoughts, words, and deeds, for one is truly the most virtuous of choices while the other is not.

30.4: When these two spirits come to a confrontation, one must decide on that eternal question: To choose life and growth or the opposite? With this, one must decide on how they will align until the end: Will they choose to align to Druj and deceit, in the worst of all existences, or will they be the Ashavans for whom enlightenment awaits?

30.5: When it comes to these two spirits, the one empowered by Druj will always choose to act against virtue in horrible ways but the other spirit, prosperous and blessed, clothed in virtue as if it were armor composed of the hardest diamonds, chooses Asha alongside all those who join the spirit on the path of devotion to satisfy that Ahura who only acts with Asha, our Mazda.

30.6: The Daevas, who give in to their delusions when they take counsel, cannot seem to choose the truly virtuous of the two and thus end up choosing the worst thought that comes to them, through which they gather with Aeshma, who curses mortals through his nature so that they may poison what is.

30.7: Those who approach the choice with the aid of Asha, Vohu Manah, and Xshatra will see themselves granted a strong and harmonious form and Armaiti will bless them with healthy breathing so that then we may shackle the Daevas within and without so what exists will be enriched by the realm that came before all others.

30.8: Oh Ahura Mazda, when the time comes for them to atone for their misdeeds arrives, we shall, through Xshatra and Vohu Manah, ask that you provide for their atonement, and then shall the earned rewards be announced to those, who have brought those empowered by Druj towards the path of Asha.

30.9: We thus desire to be those who will bring magnificence to what exists, Oh Mazda and you other Ahuras, alongside the renovators and Asha, when we have centered our thoughts wherever wisdom and understanding may be found.

30.10: Destruction comes with and towards those who embrace and empower Druj. The fastest steeds, who will have renown bestowed upon them, will be gathered, and raced towards the blessed home of Vohu Manah and of Mazda and of Asha.

30.11: Listen, all of you mortals, and learn that when you have mastered the teachings which Mazda has bestowed upon us, which speak of furtherance and stagnancy, and when the methods to combat those aligned to Druj have been mastered, alongside the methods for empowering those aligned to Asha, then all that one desires shall be provided through the blessings that come from such mastery.

Yasna 31

31.1: Now that we have learned your teachings, we will endeavor to speak the words that they refuse to hear, they who by aligning themselves to Druj seek to bring destruction to the gatherings of all those aligned to Asha, and yet these words which we hold dear are a blessing to those who have faith in Mazda.

31.2: If they cannot see the better path to journey on, then I come to you all and let you know that the Ahura, through which we can live aligned to Asha, knows the fate of those two twins.

31.3: You provide contentment through spirit and flames, and further bring equilibrium through Asha, and so we plead, Oh Mazda, that you enlighten us, we who are responsible with the knowledge provided through your majesty, with your divine words so that I may welcome all the living.

31.4: When Mazda, and the rest of the Ahuras, have sent forward Asha, Ashi, and Armaiti, whose natures call for worship, then will I attempt to gain with the aid of my virtuous mind the empowerment and strength promised to me as the way in which we will defeat those aligned to Druj.

31.5: Oh Mazda, speak to me of the ascended path, which through Asha you are the one who has made it mine, so it may be clearly perceived, and so that I may remember what I have learned through the aid of Vohu Manah and the visions I have received, which speak of what will not be and what shall be.

31.6: That which is best of all will be given to those who are enlightened, who declare for me the manthras which bring the attention of Asha, Haurvatat, and Ameretat, and Xshatra, which is of Mazda, who shall expand it with the aid of Vohu Manah, which is of him.

31.7: He, who was before what is, spoke the words conceived in his mind as thus: "May the blessed realms know the comforts of the light!" and the Creator emanated Asha from his mind. That spirit which supports the enlightened minds, by which you, Oh Ahura Mazda, further develop yet remain of an unchangeable and eternal nature.

31.8: I realize that you, who was before what is, are a dispenser of fresh wisdom, Oh Mazda, you who are the father of enlightenment, who when my eyes perceive you, I see as the source of Asha, the Ahura who is aware of all our actions.

31.9: Armaiti is of you, just as the enlightened one who designed the cow is of you, Oh Ahura Mazda, that cow whose future was made clear through alignment with the spirit, so that she could choose between the herder and those who do not care for the herd.

31.10: She chose as her master, from these two, the herder, who is enlightened and charitable, who can increase her herd. Meanwhile, no matter how much the one that does not care for the herd wails, they continue to be known for their lack of virtue.

31.11: Oh Mazda, it was you that designed for us what we were, our herds, and the spiritual teachings, through your enlightened mind and those of others, when you fashioned life into its physical form, when you made manifest the rites and the proclamations, through which one wanting their desire made manifest exercises their will freely.

31.12: Whether one speaks simply or with subterfuge, with a yell, or with wisdom or ignorance, with their heart and mind, and they seek Armaiti, then Armaiti will enlighten the spirit that calls to her.

31.13: Oh Mazda, whether their thoughts have been revealed or kept hidden, whether two conspire or commit even the smallest injury, you are aware for in your shining eyes Asha reflects all and it is you that knows if penance awaits them.

31.14: Oh Ahura, tell me of what is coming and yet may come, of the potency of the blessings that will come from Asha, and even of the curses that will come from Druj, for I wish to know how they will come when all has been reckoned with.

31.15: Oh Ahura, this I ask: What reprimand awaits those who surrender the aid Xshatra provides them to the ones aligned to Druj, those against virtue, who cannot seem to live without needing to harm both mortals and cattle unlike the honest herder?

31.16: Oh Ahura Mazda, this I ask: When will we see those who seek to spread the teachings and align their homes, with the aid of Xshatra, the provinces in which they reside, and the nations of the land to Asha? When will they who are in harmony with you come to us and how?

31.17: Who is more convincing, the Ashavan or the Drujvan? May the wise make many others wise as well. May those who revel in their ignorance see their efforts to delude others thwarted. Oh Ahura Mazda, we implore you to enlighten us.

31.18: May none of those truly devoted to the ways of Druj reach us with manthras and teachings. They will use their delusions to bring our houses, towns, provinces, and the nations of the land to a ruinous state. The recourse for them is our resistance.

31.19: Oh Ahura Mazda, you who heals what exists and are the wise source of Asha, know that he has heard you, he who wills his words to be simple and harmonious, who speaks them before crimson Atar, so that the blessings may be shared by all.

31.20: If one comes to the Ashavan, they shall be gifted with magnificent blessings and spared all tears. Oh Drujvans, you have brought to yourself through your own actions and willful spiritual ignorance a life choked by darkness, rotten food, and misery.

31.21: The Ahura, in unity with Ameretat and Haurvatat, bestow from their palace where Asha and Xshatra are found, enlightenment as pleasing as the fat of an animal to those who are sworn to them in spirit and deed.

31.22: Glory awaits the one who is charitable and supports them with their own thoughts. It is through virtuous Xshatra that they center Asha in their words and deeds. Oh Ahura Mazda, surely, they are the ones who you will treat as most welcome guests.

Yasna 32

32.1: Oh you Daevas, our families plead during my recital, with the aid of Airyaman and our clans, for Ahura Mazda's favor thusly: "Let us our homes be yours. You sunder those who hate you."

32.2: To us, Ahura Mazda, who is in unity with Vohu Manah, and is a constant friend to those who shine with Asha, answers with authority thusly: "We align with those who welcome Armaiti and are thus blessed with prosperity. Let them be with us."

32.3: Oh you Daevas, all of you, are but saplings grown from unvirtuous thought, alongside those self-declared masters who worship you and act aligned to Druj and scornful ways, all for which you have been consistently reviled in all of the seven realms of the world.

32.4: You, Daevas, manifest horrors by providing mortals with ways to develop into your servants, thereby causing them to be scared of enlightenment thus fleeing from Asha and the wisdom of Ahura Mazda.

32.5: This is how you, the Daevas, trick mortals and divert them from virtuous living and the blessings of Ameretat, for it is through that unvirtuous spirit and unvirtuous thinking, along with unvirtuous words and the actions they inspire, that one may be able to recognize a Drujvan with authority.

32.6: Countless have the crimes against peace been for which they are reviled: whether they continue this path or not it is you, Oh Ahura Mazda, who knows that through your enlightened thinking what the result of the actions of the people will be. Our adoration of you will be heard by all, along with our adoration of Asha, which is strong through Xshatra, who is of you.

32.7: Oh Ahura Mazda, in full honesty I make it clear that I know of no desire to engage in such violent crimes, and if I do may I be reviled only after undergoing the trial of the molten metal, in which you know the nature of all things.

32.8: For it was Yima, son of Vivahvan, who was reviled for his crimes against the cattle and the people, which he attempted to please through his actions, in the eyes of the divine. Oh Mazda, when it comes to any such crimes, it is your decision that matters.

32.9: When the unvirtuous speak, they taint not just how they are perceived but also taint the minds of the living. They desecrate the duty of the enlightened. Oh Mazda and Asha, hear of these troubles which plague my spirit.

32.10: When they speak their horrid words, they taint how they are perceived and cannot gaze upon the cattle with their unvirtuous eyes just as they cannot witness the light of the sun. They corrupt those who walk in justice and turn them into servants of those who walk with Druj, and steal from the food supplies, and strike against those aligned to Asha.

32.11: Oh Mazda, they seek to ruin life itself, these Drujvans of all genders who brag about their greatness, about desecrating our heritage, they are the ones who tear those aligned to Asha away from enlightenment.

32.12: They speak in ways that make mortals cast aside their best deeds, and it is Mazda then who speaks with offense against those who harm the cattle, for they influence the Karapan to proceed towards the ways of Graehma and those with power aligned to Druj instead of towards Asha.

32.13: Oh Mazda, though they believe it is through Xshatra, Graehma's clan makes their home in the palace of ignorance, with the corrupters of what exists, who desire naught but to curse the clan of your advocate and block them from perceiving Asha.

32.14: The Kavis, supporters of Graehma, shackle their minds and their dignities day after day by supporting this Drujvan, who calls for the sacrifice of the cattle so that they may make themselves drunk with the power of the exquisite flames.

32.15: Both the Karapans and Kavis have lost themselves through this, for they wish to control what they fear will control them. It will come to the notice of those two who reside in the palace of enlightenment.

32.16: Oh Ahura Mazda, there is a blessing beyond compare and you know of it, for you take pleasure in raising up the pious, and it is you who has the power over all my fears, and knowing the crimes of the Drujvan, make that blessing manifest which empowers us all.

Yasna 33

33.1: The Master, who was before what is, decides as a Ratu between those who align to Druj and those who align to Asha, and even those who are on the upright path for they shall have their flaws measured alongside their merits.

33.2: Just as the Drujvan works through their words or thoughts or deeds, there are those who work through virtue and hospitality, and it is they that answer the call of Ahura Mazda and reside within the pleasure of his will.

33.3: Oh Ahura, whether their virtue is exemplified through Airyaman in their families or their clans, or by their eager care of the cattle, they are the ones who shall reside in the fields of Asha where enlightenment is found.

33.4: Oh Mazda, I pray and cast away ignorance and impetuousness from your sight, along with hatred of one's family and the Druj uncovered by Airyaman, also those who hate their clan and provide scornful advice on how to treat the cattle.

33.5: Even in my slumber I seek the glories that come from Sraosha, I who am now old yet am enlightened through Xshatra, as is right for taking the path of Asha towards where Mazda resides.

33.6: I am a Zaotar, upright with Asha. Thus, right with this virtuous spirit, pleasure fills me when these thoughts arrive due to the care I provide through my own deeds. Oh Ahura Mazda, this said, I implore you to provide your visions and counsel.

33.7: Oh, glorious beings, come to me. Oh Mazda, come to me, present and bold, with Asha and Vohu Manah who listen to what I say above all other of the sacrificers. Bestow upon us all brilliant manifestations that will fill us with inspiration and veneration.

33.8: Oh Mazda, take note of my reasonings, and that I seek them with the aid of Vohu Manah, and provide you through Asha with worship and praise. Ameretat and Haurvatat are your offerings through which we achieve harmony.

33.9: Oh Mazda, an enlightened being will bring you that spirit, which in conflict with the other, is developing further through Asha, and brings the highest bliss and comfort. There will come a time when these spirits, whose souls are not distant, will be truly united.

33.10: Oh Mazda, so that all the bounties will be accessible, those who have been, are, and will be, may they be blessed with your consent. May Asha, Vohu Manah, and Xshatra be empowered through your essence as is hoped for.

33.11: Oh Mazda, most powerful of the Ahura, and with Armaiti and Asha supporting our herds in your authority, along with Vohu Manah, hear me and be merciful towards me at all moments!

33.12: Oh Ahura Mazda, come towards me and display your might through the power of Armaiti, through that most enriched of spirits, and may swiftness be given to you as is right, with the advancing mastery expanded through Asha and all joyous things through Vohu Manah.

33.13: You, whose sight is unencumbered, support us. Oh Ahura, display to me all the manifestations of Xshatra and Ashi through which we are enlightened. Oh bountiful Armaiti, may we learn the spiritual teachings through Asha.

33.14: Zarathushtra, as a gift, offers Mazda the strength of his body, his prestigious enlightenment, and his Ashavic deeds, and to the pronouncement of Sraosha and to Xshatra.

Yasna 34

34.1:   Oh Ahura Mazda, Ameretat, Asha, and Haurvatat are of you, through the words, deeds, and worship you accept from what is being offered to you, by as many of us as possible.

34.2:   Oh Mazda, all forms of the virtuous spirit are developed from your thoughts, along with the deeds of the prosperous ones whose souls are aligned with Asha, and we welcome all praise and adoration due to you who keeps our herds with our trust.

34.3:   Oh Ahura Mazda, as the sacrificial offering that is due to you and to Asha, we provide with reverence, through Xshatra, all our herds, which we have fed through the aid of Vohu Manah. Oh Mazda, it is so that the charitable shall be granted the blessings promised by you and all such as you.

34.4:   Oh Ahura Mazda, we desire Atar, empowered by Asha, strong and forceful, to be a radiant aid to your devotee, and for your enemy a source of injury.

34.5:   Oh Mazda, will Xshatra, who is of you, through which I answer your summons, protect me in my deeds and even when I sleep, me, your pitiable supporter, who aligns to Asha and Vohu Manah? It is we who proclaim that you are greater than all the beasts, whether they be Daevas or even mortals.

34.6:   Oh Mazda, make your true nature clear to me through Asha and Vohu Manah, every day of my life, so that I may find you once more, and, filled with joy, bring you even more worship and praise.

34.7:   Oh Mazda, where are those ones who are so spirited in their knowledge of the blessings and legacies which enlightenment brings that they can transmute anxiety and misfortune into pleasure? In all honestly, I know of no other that can protect us as you can, so do so.

34.8: Oh Mazda, it is so that we are feared due to the ways you forcefully strike against those who would harm us, as one who is mighty bests a weaker opponent. If they do not center their thoughts on Asha, then there is no need to keep Vohu Manah close to them.

34.9: Oh Mazda, these unvirtuous actors who, ignorant of enlightenment, will cast aside the blessings of Armaiti, who is esteemed by your thoughts, and their masters will treat Asha as they treat the wild beasts and cast them away as well.

34.10: Oh Ahura Mazda, the enlightened one speaks of enlightened action and of blessed Armaiti, knowing that they are the creative companion of Asha, and of all the wards of protection which you provide through Xshatra, who is of you.

34.11: Oh Mazda, Haurvatat and Ameretat nourish us both. Through the enlightenment provided by Xshatra, we cause Armaiti and Asha to develop further in harmony and might. It is with them that you make our enemies cower.

34.12: What do you consider a prayer? What do you desire? What method of praise or worship? Oh Mazda, declare it to us who listen so that we may also know what blessings come from prayer. Focus our sight on the path of Asha, which for the enlightened is the most pleasant of journeys.

34.13: Oh Ahura Mazda, this is the way that you have declared to me to be the enlightened one, beautifully decorated with the spiritual teachings by which your supporters walk with Asha, towards that treasure promised to the charitable, that treasure which is you.

34.14: Oh Ahura Mazda, it is so and, as such, desirable that you provide this to the mortal living for their enlightened deeds, as you reside with the fruitful cow, and it is through your virtuous insight that we align to Asha and spread enlightenment in our communities.

34.15: Oh Ahura Mazda, tell me of all that is blessed, of both the deeds and tributes, of those in concert with Vohu Manah, and who are empowered through their praise by Asha. It is through Xshatra, who is of you, that the brilliant existence that I imagine becomes manifest.

The Yasna Haptanghaiti

Yasna 35

35.1: *We worship Ahura Mazda, the Ashavan and source of Asha. We worship the Amesha Spenta, their virtuous authority, of they who are the charitable ones. We worship the whole of the material and spiritual realms of those aligned to Asha, with adoration for virtuous Asha, and with adoration for the virtuous spiritual teachings of Mazdayasna.*

35.2: We are the praisers of what is virtuously thought, of what is virtuously spoken, and of what is virtuously done, whether now and here or then and later, for we aim to not ill-treat what is virtuous.

35.3: Oh Ahura Mazda, who through Asha is made beautiful, we choose you so that we may imagine, pronounce, and do those deeds that surpass what is in both the realms.

35.4: Through these magnificent deeds, we plead towards those who listen and those who do not, towards those who are strong and those who are not, that they set peace in its place and fields for the cattle.

35.5: To you, as much as we can, we declare and provide what we have gained from Xshatra to Ahura Mazda, the most magnificent master, and to Asha Vahishta.

35.6: Those of any gender, who seek to know the truth, should let it grow in them like a rich grain seed, and let this growth be known to those who wish to grow as well.

35.7: For we have learned that worship and praise of Ahura Mazda for the fields of the cattle are, to you, wonderful. Thus, we wish to do this for you and let all under our instruction know of this.

35.8: He has made it so that all that are that wish to find the sweet refuge of Asha may find it within the embrace of Asha in both realms.

35.9: Oh Ahura Mazda, we wish to declare, through our utmost veneration, the Ashavic nature of our declarations and words. We have chosen you to listen to us and to teach us.

35.10: Oh Ahura, through these words and united with the enlightenment provided through Asha and virtuous Xshatra, and with boundless praise and grand declarations, we provide this worship unmatched by any other worship.

Yasna 36

36.1: Oh Ahura Mazda, we, this community of Atar, approach you and attend to your most bountiful spirit, which the harmful ones view as the source of their pain.

36.2: Oh Atar of Ahura Mazda, you who are so wonderful, join us and provide us with the finest of blessings, those that delight the one that is most delightful, and with reverence for the one that deserves the most reverence

36.3: You are truly Atar of Ahura Mazda! You are truly his most bountiful spirit! Oh Atar of Ahura Mazda, we attend to you with the most enlivening of your names.

36.4: We attend to you, Vohu Manah, to you virtuous Asha, to you with our enlightened deeds and words.

36.5: Oh Ahura Mazda, we adore and enliven you. We attend to you with every virtuous thought, with every virtuous word, with every virtuous deed.

36.6: Oh Ahura Mazda, we declare that out of all the lights that are, it is this one that is the most beautiful, and has been since the highest of them all, known as Hvare.

Yasna 37

37.1: Thus, we worship Ahura Mazda, who formed the cattle and Asha, and formed the Apas and the lovely plants, and formed the lights and the earth and all that is virtuous.

37.2: Due to Xshatra, who is of him, and his magnificence and artistry, we worship him with the most prominent worship that we, who live in harmony with the cattle, can provide.

37.3: We worship Mazda with the Ahuric titles most dear and bountiful to him. We worship him from deep in our bones and with the fullness of our strength. We worship him and the Fravashis of the Ashavans of all genders.

37.4: We worship Asha Vahishta, who is beyond beautiful and bountiful, immortal and shining bright, and the most virtuous.

37.5: We also worship Vohu Manah and virtuous Xshatra and the virtuous Mazdayasnian spiritual teachings and the joy that comes from virtue and virtuous Armaiti.

Yasna 38

38.1: Oh Ahura Mazda, we worship Zam and all women, they who carry us, and who are yours. We worship those who are worthily chosen in harmony with Asha.

38.2: The libations, ablutions, enlightenment, and Armaiti: We worship them alongside virtuous Ashi, the virtuous renewal, the virtuous offering of the fat, virtuous praise, and virtuous blessings.

38.3: We worship the Apas, delicious and satisfying, who are the Ahuranis that, due to the artistry of the Ahura, flow forth. We provide for, in both realms, you who provide us with safe passage, who flow wonderfully, and are a pleasure to swim among.

38.4: Naming those names which Ahura Mazda, who is the provider of what is virtuous, has given to you when you were formed by him, oh virtuous ones, we thus worship you with them, we praise you with them, we revere you with them, and we enliven you with them.

38.5:   Apas, we address you now, along with the fruitful mothers, who should not be killed for they provide succor to the poor and quench the thirst of all beings and are virtuous and most beautiful. You are the virtuous ones, who come to us with far-reaching charity, you are the providers, you are the pleasant ones, you who are mothers, you who are treasured.

Yasna 39

39.1:   Hereby we now worship the soul of the cow along with the one that fashioned her. As well, our own souls, and those of our animals to which we have granted domestic refuge, whether they belong to others or to us.

39.2:   We also worship the souls of the wild and harmless animals. We worship the souls of the Ashavans of any gender no matter where they are from, for their spiritual teachings are magnificent and will prevail as they have for eternity.

39.3:   Hereby we now worship the virtuous Amesha Spenta of any gender, who are immortal and ever thriving, and remain in a state of enlightenment.

39.4:   Oh Ahura Mazda, since you conceived, and declared, and formed, and work through all that is virtuous, we thus offer our dedication and worship to you, Oh Ahura Mazda, and thus revitalize you.

39.5:   We attend to you with our familial brethren, for they are virtuous, and with virtuous Asha, who brings us virtue and joy, and virtuous Armaiti.

Yasna 40

40.1:   Oh Ahura Mazda, during our offerings, grant us the bounty of your wisdom, which through your charity will take form. Oh Ahura Mazda, this is that stalwart bounty which you have presented through the spiritual teachings:

40.2: You will grant us that which is of both realms, this one and the spiritual one, so that through it we may achieve your Ashavic fellowship for eternity.

40.3: Oh Ahura Mazda, you will grant us men who are united with Asha, who love Asha, and are virtuous herders by their natures, so that we will have long-lasting, abundant, and unending fellowship with those who both give to us and receive from us.

40.4: Thus, may these be the families, the communities, the fellowships, which we follow. Oh Ahura Mazda, thus may we be in your favor, the Ashavans, who will be heartily blessed with what we wish for.

Yasna 41

41.1: We offer welcoming praise and adoration which we sing and declare to Ahura Mazda and Asha Vahishta.

41.2: Oh Ahura Mazda, may we attain Xshatra, who is of you, for eternity. Oh, may we only experience the rule of a virtuous ruler in both realms, you who are the most charitable one among all that are.

41.3: We choose you, the blessed and abundant Yazata, who is in harmony with Asha. Oh, thus may you be the center of our lives and bodies in both realms, you who are the most charitable one among all that are.

41.4: Oh Ahura Mazda, may we deserve and earn your long-lasting aid, and may we become spirited and ardent through you. Oh, may you aid us for as long as we wish for, you who are the most charitable one among all that are.

41.5: Oh Ahura Mazda, we have made it known that we are your praisers and manthrans, for we are willing, and we will position ourselves thusly. Oh Ahura Mazda, this is that stalwart bounty which you have presented through the spiritual teachings:

41.6: You will grant us that which is of both realms, this one and the spiritual one, so that through it we may attain your refuge and that of Asha for eternity.

41.7: They that are, who are of any gender, Ahura Mazda knows through Asha of their glorious sacrifices: Thus, we offer them worship! (x2) *Of virtuous thoughts, of virtuous words, and of virtuous deeds, in all places and those that have happened and have yet to happen, we welcome such virtuous acts!* (x2) Worthy and chosen through Asha are they, the Ratus throughout the world, who bring enlightenment to the world, through deeds done on behalf of Ahura Mazda, who has become the advocate of the impoverished. (x4) Asha is virtuous and magnificent, and joy upon joy is what Asha provides, for thus is Asha Vahishta. (x3)

41.8: *We worship the Yasna Haptanghaiti, the mighty one, filled with Asha, and the source of Asha!* They that are, who are of any gender, Ahura Mazda knows through Asha of their glorious sacrifices: Thus, we offer them worship!

The Ushtavaiti Gatha

Yasna 43

43.1: It is my desire that strength and harmony come as a blessing to those whom Ahura Mazda, through the authority of his will, grants their desires. Oh Armaiti, I wish to have the power of Asha bestowed upon me, from which I will receive from Ashi riches and enlightenment.

43.2: Oh Mazda, may those who seek comfort find the greatest comfort, which can be recognized through the aid of Spenta Mainyu, from which they will receive the blessings of enlightenment through Asha, along with a joyous and long life throughout all their days.

43.3: He who shows us the greatest and most upright of all paths which brings blessings to both the physical and mental realms, that one of Asha full of fortune, where one of the Ahura is found, who is spirited and is like you, Oh Mazda, familiar and bountiful.

43.4: Oh Mazda, I will believe that you are fearless and bountiful when, through Ashi, you dispense what is yours to those aligned to Druj and those aligned to Asha as is due to them, and through the blazing Atar who is empowered by Asha, who shall bring me the greatness that is enlightenment.

43.5: Oh Ahura Mazda, I know that you are bountiful and, when I perceive you, you who were before what is, who set what is in its place, I know that you place value on our deeds and words, where the unvirtuous of them receive as they provide, and the virtuous are blessed by Ashi, with your prowess, at the completion of the renovation of all that is.

43.6: This renovation, where you and Spenta Mainyu will be present, where you Mazda will display the strongest

Xshatra, it is there, due to Vohu Manah gathering the herds through the call of Asha, that Armaiti declares the enlightened decisions, which none can deny, that you have made for all.

43.7: Oh Ahura Mazda, I know that you are bountiful when you ask me such enlightened questions: "Who are you? Who do you belong to? When will you, who are so zealous, question your own life and your possessions?"

43.8: To you, I reply thus: "To start off, Zarathushtra. I, an honest man, search for all enemies of the Drujvan, and I see myself as the stalwart supporter of the Ashavan, and I wish for the riches that one such as me deserves, who with the fullness of my authority and will, praises and glorifies you, Oh Mazda."

43.9: Oh Ahura Mazda, I know that you are bountiful when you ask me such enlightened questions: "Who is that you seek this knowledge for?" I reply thus: "It is for Atar, who aids me in my pondering as how to best provide blessings to those who revere Asha, which is how I most wish to use my skills."

43.10: Show me Asha, which I plead for, which I will reach with the aid of Armaiti, and then ask us any questions you wish. I know you are eager to question me and you, who are both spirited and eager, have the authority to do so.

43.11: Oh Ahura Mazda, I know that you are bountiful when you enlighten me in such a way. It is through your words that I have learned about what was before what is. Aid me in doing these great things you ask of me, for the mortals among me are dismayed by what I confidently say.

43.12: "Your insight will lead you to Asha," you say to me, and set me on this mission which I shall not stray from. Let me stand upright before Sraosha, who walks with me,

39

accompanied by Ashi who enriches me, for it is Ashi who will be most charitable when the time comes to provide to each according to their records.

43.13: Oh Ahura Mazda, I know that you are bountiful when you enlighten me in such a way, taking note of what I desire. Of this you have informed me: Though none compels you to do so, you provide, through Xshatra, who is of you, a long life, and the treasures I desire.

43.14: Oh Mazda, you who are prosperous beyond compare, grant your support and insight to me who you have welcomed as a friend, which you provide through Xshatra, who is of you, to those aligned to Asha. Let me and all those who learn the manthras stand upright against the opponents of your words.

43.15: Oh Ahura Mazda, I know that you are bountiful when you enlighten me in such a way. It is through the practice of Tushna Matai that I find myself most pleased. None should try to please all those aligned to Druj for they claim falsely that they are aligned to Asha.

43.16: Oh Ahura, I, who am Zarathushtra, will always choose that most bountiful spirit of yours. Oh Mazda, may Asha be made manifest, strong and full of vigor, blessed by the light of the sun. May Armaiti grant me what comes through Xshatra and may Ashi inspire me towards enlightened deeds.

Yasna 44

44.1: Oh Ahura, I ask you this in the simplest way possible: Oh Mazda, as I am most worshipful towards you, let me, your friend, know the best ways to worship you. Let Asha unite us all into a society bound by friendship so that we may truly welcome Vohu Manah.

44.2: Oh Ahura, I ask you this in the simplest way possible: That realm that was before what is, what is it like? Oh

Mazda, you are the source, bountiful in Asha, who notes spiritually the accounts of all, you who heals all that is, our foremost ally.

44.3: Oh Ahura, I ask you this in the simplest way possible: He who was before all that is, the father of Asha, who set all that is in its course, who is this? Who was it that set the course of the sun and stars? Who is it that causes the moon to wax and wane? I desire to know of these matters and others, Oh Mazda.

44.4: Oh Ahura, I ask you this in the simplest way possible: Who has set the sky and Zam in their places? Who has developed plant life and set the Apas on their course? Who provides much swiftness to Vata and the clouds? Oh Mazda, who is the source of enlightenment?

44.5: Oh Ahura, I ask you this in the simplest way possible: Who is the artist that fashioned both light and darkness? Who is the artist that fashioned sleep and the waking hours? Who fashioned dawn, noon, and dusk, all which remind responsible beings of their duties?

44.6: Oh Ahura, I ask you, in the simplest way possible, if these words of mine are correct: Armaiti allows us, through our deeds, to unite with Asha who enlightens us through Xshatra, who is of you. For whom, though, did you fashion the fruitful cattle from which we gain such joy?

44.7: Oh Ahura, I ask you this in the simplest way possible: Who, through Xshatra, fashioned blessed Armaiti? Who actively provides fathers with such excellent sons? Oh Mazda, knowing these answers is how I, gifted with this insight, will support you, alongside Spenta Mainyu, with whom you made all that is.

44.8: Oh Ahura Mazda, I ask you this in the simplest way possible, so that I may remember your advice, as well as all your declarations which have enlightened me and those which Asha will provide, regarding the course of all that is: What is the path that my soul must take so that I may know only the greatest of all things to come?

44.9: Oh Ahura, I ask you this in the simplest way possible: How will the Master, filled of Xshatra, let me know the spiritual teachings with which I, who am most charitable, may purify myself through the grand and spirited Xshatra in whose palace resides Asha and Vohu Manah, Oh Mazda?

44.10: Oh Ahura, I ask you this in the simplest way possible: Tell me of the spiritual teachings which, among all of them, is the best for aligning with Asha and supporting my herds: Oh Mazda, does my spirited insight, provided by you, see that simple answer through which my deeds are inspired by the teachings of Armaiti?

44.11: Oh Ahura, I ask you this in the simplest way possible: Oh Mazda, how will Armaiti reach those who dispense your spiritual teachings? I, though I am the first to support you, am not alone. My spirit is alienated from those who do not support you.

44.12: Oh Ahura, I ask you this in the simplest way possible: Who speaks through Asha? The ones I keep in my counsel or those aligned to Druj? Which of these is it? Which one seeks to harm me? Is it the former or the latter that seeks to cast away your blessings? Obviously, it is the latter, not the former, for they intend nothing but harm.

44.13: Oh Ahura, I ask you this in the simplest way possible: How do we drive away Druj from ourselves, and cast away those who are not supportive, and do not seek the benevolence of Asha nor care for any enlightened advice?

44.14: Oh Ahura, I ask you this in the simplest way possible: How do I transform Druj into Asha? Let me use your manthras and teachings to be swift in this action. Oh Mazda, strike eagerly against those aligned to Druj, for they are poisoned and cursed.

44.15: Oh Ahura, I ask you this, hoping for you to use your authority to make Asha my shield, in the simplest way possible: Oh Mazda, when there are two forces in conflict with each other over what you have declared and wish to make manifest, which of the two forces will you bless with victory?

44.16: Oh Ahura, I ask you this in the simplest way possible: Through your declarations, will you assign Verethragna to protect the living? Oh, healer of all that is, make the decision to shine blessings upon my home. Oh Mazda, let Sraosha come with Vohu Manah to anyone you deem worthy.

44.17: Oh Ahura, I ask you this in the simplest way possible: Oh Mazda, how do I reach that goal, which you and I both share, which is of you, and how may my voice be so spirited as to adorn, and as to be as a dwelling, to both Haurvatat and Ameretat, through the Ashavic manthras?

44.18: Oh Ahura, I ask you this in the simplest way possible: Oh Mazda, have I earned through Asha these treasures, of ten mares and a stallion, and a camel, through which I can be as you are and be one with Haurvatat and Ameretat?

44.19: Oh Ahura, I ask you this in the simplest way possible: Say there is one who will not give these treasures to he who deserves it, who then must obtain them through such simple words: Will he be chastised for this action in the realm that was before what is? I believe I know the final answer of what will happen.

44.20: Oh Mazda, has there even been a Daeva that has used their authority in a virtuous manner? What of the Karapans and Usijs who sacrifice the cow to Aeshma, under the authority of their unpleasant declarations, and what of the Kavis that demand lamentations in their rites? They do not support the cow or bring her towards the fields of Asha.

Yasna 45

45.1: I make a proclamation, so listen to me, hear me now, all of you wherever you may be. See all that is and note how brilliant it is. May what is now never be sundered again by those who revel in spiritual confusion, the Drujvans, through unvirtuous decisions welcomed through their own words.

45.2: I make a proclamation on those two spirits in the realm before what is where the bountiful one says thus to the one that brings destruction: "Our thoughts, our words, our minds, our decisions, our declarations, our deeds, our spiritual views, and our souls, are not in harmony."

45.3: I make a proclamation about what is as Ahura Mazda, who knows all, explained to me thus: "They shall know the extent of misery for they cast aside the lessons of the manthras as I have developed and taught them."

45.4: I make a proclamation on the most glorious of what is. Oh Mazda, in unity with Asha, I am familiar with who set in place what is, the source of enlightenment, the father of Armaiti whose deeds are virtuous. None can fool this Ahura, for they are omniscient.

45.5: I make a proclamation, which I was told by the one who is most bountiful, on those words which are most glorious for mortals to hear. Those who follow the ways of Sraosha will be united with Haurvatat and Ameretat. Ahura Mazda will remember the deeds done in accord with the most virtuous of spirits.

45.6: I make a proclamation, on the most magnificent of all, that those who are most charitable to their fellows should be praised as is right by Asha. Ahura Mazda, with Spenta Mainyu, is always listening. I want him to teach me of the magnificence of his enlightened ways, he who alongside Vohu Manah I seek advice from and who I shower with praise.

45.7: Blessed by the bounty that will be provided, that of they who truly are, have been, and will be, they make the soul of one aligned to Asha empowered and harmonized by Ameretat, which confuses those aligned to Druj. Through Xshatra, Ahura Mazda sets all that is.

45.8: We, who try to welcome him with our most reverent praises, know that I have witnessed him, Ahura Mazda, for it is through Asha that I am a witness to the deeds and declarations of the virtuous spirit. It is for him that we bring our praises to that most welcoming palace.

45.9: We aim to support, with the aid of Vohu Manah, he who through his will can be a source of blessings lest we seek the source of curses. May Ahura Mazda, through Xshatra, keep us refreshed so that we can support our fellows and our cattle as we are familiar with the enlightenment Asha provides.

45.10: We aim to provide worship to Armaiti and that Ahura known to all as Mazda. When one, through Asha and Vohu Manah, has committed themselves to Xshatra, who is of him, they gain from him Haurvatat and Ameretat along with might and harmony as they are of him.

45.11: That one who, true to him, has decided to cast away the Daevas and those mortals who hate him, and stands with those whose deeds speak of their virtue and alignment towards him: It is through the spiritual teachings of that charitable master, Oh Ahura Mazda, that they become Saoshyants and as allies, brothers, and fathers.

Yasna 46

46.1: What land will provide me with succor? Where will I go to find it? They know not family and clan, or Airyaman who I am with, and they do not please me nor do the tyrants who rule it for they are aligned to Druj. Oh Ahura Mazda, how can I even please you?

46.2: Oh Mazda, I know why I am so powerless. I have so little cattle and I am but one among few brethren. Oh Ahura, I lament to you and ask you to view me favorably to support me as friends support each other. Look after our strength, we who are enlightened by Asha.

46.3: Oh Mazda, when will we rise like bulls at sunrise above all that is so that Asha may be in reach with more declarations, we who are enlightened Saoshyants? Who are the ones that will be nourished by Vohu Manah as if fed with the fat of the animals? Oh Ahura, I beg of you to tell me.

46.4: Those aligned to Druj seek to prevent those bulls from rising beyond the districts and provinces, from promulgating the words of Asha, they who curse us and are displeased even with their own deeds. Oh Mazda, make these bulls the masters of the spread of this glorious knowledge, and be the one who will deprive those aligned to Druj of the blessings of Xshatra and their livelihoods.

46.5: Oh Ahura Mazda, if a ruler were to harbor them and give them rest and refreshment, and make them promises under Mithra's watch, an Ashavan, upright and making fair judgments, should tell their family of them, who are aligned to Druj, so that they may be shielded against all attacks.

46.6: If they, however, do not come seeking succor, let them instead find whatever else they seek in the palace of Druj. One who is full of Druj will welcome those aligned to Druj just as an Ashavan will treat as a friend one aligned to Asha, as it has been set by your spiritual teachings since before what is, Oh Ahura.

46.7: Oh Mazda, who do you assign to guard me against those aligned to Druj when they try to take and injure me, other than your enlightened Atar, whose deeds empower Asha. Oh Ahura, aid me in understanding your spiritual teachings on this matter.

46.8: If someone aims to attack my herds, may I be protected from their destructive deeds. Oh Mazda, may their deeds reflect upon them and wrack them with hostility, for in this way do they live a life not worth living and they aggressively prevent themselves from living a better life.

46.9: Who is spirited enough to be my first students in the knowledge that you have so swiftly imparted upon me, you who are most bountiful in your deeds, the Ahuric Ashavan? For this knowledge is what he who fashioned the cow brings through Asha, and speaks to Asha, of one who will enliven me, with the aid of Vohu Manah.

46.10: Oh Ahura Mazda, this person of any gender, who will provide for me that which you know to be most excellent, given by Ashi through Vohu Manah on behalf of Xshatra through Asha, and who I will encourage to praise all those who are with you: It is with those, after all, that I cross the Chinvat Bridge.

46.11: The Karapans and Kavis pervert what they receive from Xshatra to force mortals to engage in disgraceful deeds to poison what is. Their own souls, and even the spiritual teachings they have learned, will flee from them when they reach the Chinvat Bridge, where they choose to remain until the accounting as guests of the palace of Druj.

46.12: When he, Ahura Mazda, advances with Asha alongside the honored brethren, such as the descendants of Tura, son of Friya, supporting with zeal Armaiti's herds, he then brings them into unity with Vohu Manah, and has declared he will continue to support them.

46.13: He who has pleased Zarathushtra Spitama and granted him many treasures deserves to be honored. Ahura Mazda grants him his place in what is. For he supports the herds, aided by Vohu Manah, and we know that he sees Asha as a true friend.

46.14: Oh Zarathushtra, which Ashavan is your ally during this grand sacrifice? Who deserves to be honored? Oh Ahura Mazda, I wish it to be the Kavi Vishtaspa, so that we may share in the blessings that you bestow upon his household, along with those who answer my call towards enlightenment.

46.15: Oh Haecataspa Spitama, let your clan know that they will know what is just and what is unjust. Through their deeds they will know Asha and align themselves to that Ahura that was before what is.

46.16: Oh Frashaoshtra Hvogva, go and find those who are lively to seek those we wish to join us, to where Armaiti and Asha are one, where the enlightened are blessed through Xshatra, where the blessings of Ahura Mazda reside.

46.17: Oh Jamaspa Hvogva, this is where I will proclaim your duties, and your praises, with the one who is the blessed Sraosha, who knows what is just and unjust alongside their vigilant master, Ahura Mazda.

46.18: Oh Mazda, I promise, to he who is most suitable through Vohu Manah, all the finest things in my authority to provide, and harm to those who would harm us, and that through Asha I may please your will. This is the enlightened decision I have made.

46.19: He who is united with Asha will manifest for me, Zarathushtra, my greatest imaginings, for I deserve the treasures that elevate me to what is beyond, which in my imaginings includes two fruitful cows. Oh Mazda, it is you who seems to me to be the one in the best position to provide me this.

The Spentamainyu Gatha

Yasna 47

47.1: Alongside the enlightened Spenta Mainyu, with all deeds and words done in unity with Asha, Haurvatat and Ameretat are due to Ahura Mazda, he who knows these matters with the aid of Xshatra and Armaiti.

47.2: The most majestic deeds one does with the aid of Armaiti and that most bountiful spirit, done in search of the enlightened declarations well spoken, one does with this insight: "He is Mazda, the source of Asha."

47.3: Oh Mazda, you are the father of Spenta Mainyu, who fashioned for them the cattle which bring us so much joy, and of Armaiti, gifting her these peaceful fields, through your enlightened guidance.

47.4: Oh Mazda, those who align to Druj cast themselves away from this blessed spirit, for they are those who know not of Asha. Rich and poor alike treat the Ashavan with respect just as they do not treat the Drujvan with respect.

47.5: Oh Ahura Mazda, it is through Spenta Mainyu that you provide the Ashavan with all the treasures the Drujvan must forfeit, as they are distant from you through their own deeds, since they have chosen to count the unvirtuous as their allies.

47.6: Oh Ahura Mazda, it is through Spenta Mainyu that Atar provides for us on your behalf, harmoniously and virtuously, as we remember Armaiti and Asha, who are ever reliable. It is because of this many make their way towards you.

Yasna 48

48.1: Oh Ahura, if, when all receive what has been promised to them, Asha conquers Druj, which I have constantly known Armaiti to proclaim to mortals and Daevas alike, then one will come who will praise and bless you like no other.

48.2: Oh Ahura, enlighten me with your knowledge before the treasures I have imagined arrive for me. Oh Mazda, will the Ashavan conquer the Drujvan? This, if made manifest, will be magnificent.

48.3: Oh Mazda, enlighten all those who welcome what you, the most charitable and bountiful Ahura, teach to us through Asha, including your esoteric teachings, which you impart through virtuous enlightenment.

48.4: Oh Mazda, there are those who revel in both knowledge and ignorance and display their spiritual understanding in such a way. With deed and word, they seek nothing but what pleases them, what they desire, what they most prefer. There is no end to your knowledge, and you know such a person.

48.5: Only the virtuous, and not the corrupt, should have the right to rule. Oh Armaiti, through enlightened deeds, let only the greatest blessings purify us and the cattle, who you have multiplied to nourish us, just as we were pure at birth.

48.6: Oh, you who are known to be enlightened, know again that they do nourish our households and thus bring us harmony and might. It is you, Ahura Mazda, through Asha, since you developed what is, who has provided for them the plants.

48.7: Cast aside Aeshma! Slice your fury into pieces for it shall keep you from enlightenment. Oh Ahura, let those who ally themselves to the blessed ones be shielded by Asha, who resides in your palace.

48.8: Oh Mazda, what do you request through virtuous Xshatra, who is of you? Oh Ahura, what of the treasures you have promised me? What, through Asha, who is the most empowered even in the presence of the spirited, are the deeds that you encourage the virtuous spirits to perform?

48.9: Oh Mazda, when will I know the extent of your rule, which is through Asha, for I am terrified? Let me know, as simply as possible, your enlightened declaration on this matter so that those who are as Saoshyants will know the answer and Ashi's blessings.

48.10: Oh Mazda, when will your Manthran see those honorable people join his side? When will those intoxicated Karapans, who rack the bodies of others with discomfort through their urine-drinking ways, be kicked away along with those tyrants who rule the nations of the lands with their cursed minds?

48.11: Oh Mazda, when will Armaiti, united with Asha, come with Xshatra and provide our houses and fields with blessings? Who are they that will finally bring peace between them and those who are aligned to Druj, blood-stained as they are? Who are they that will have the insight to reach enlightenment?

48.12: Oh Mazda, they are the Saoshyants, present in all nations of the lands, who will seek to be known through their deeds, empowered by Vohu Manah and your declarations, alongside Asha. It is they who will banish Aeshma.

Yasna 49

49.1: Bendva, that chieftain, has had his fill of my barley. Oh Mazda, come to me, who aims to please the ill-herded through Asha, support me and bring me what I wish to be done: Bring his demise with the aid of Vohu Manah.

49.2: This Bendva allows a Drujvan to teach in his presence, who constantly rends the people from Asha. Oh Mazda, he does not even welcome that bountiful Armaiti nor does he even seek the wisdom of Vohu Manah.

49.3: Oh Mazda, blessings have come from Asha for our true faith, but Druj harms those who embrace the despised ways. As such, I plead for the refuge that enlightenment brings, where I banish all of those who align to Druj from our community.

49.4: The unenlightened empower Aeshma and their furious ways through their words, not supporting the care and breeding of the cattle, and by letting their unvirtuous deeds triumph since they know not of virtuous deeds, thereby through their spiritual teachings, pleasing to those aligned to Druj, they are able to manifest Daevas.

49.5: Oh Mazda, grant the one, whose spiritual knowledge finds refuge with Vohu Manah, prosperity and the fat of animals. Oh Ahura, do this for those who, through Armaiti, are familiar with Asha and all those under the watch of Xshatra, who is of you.

49.6: Oh Mazda, I beg of you, and of Asha, to speak to us of your enlightened passions, so that it is simple to discern how we can make the spiritual teachings heard, those which are from you, Oh Ahura.

49.7: Oh Mazda, let Vohu Manah aid them in hearing this! Let Asha aid them in hearing! Oh Ahura, listen! Which clan, which family, will, as requested, most honor Airyaman?

49.8: Oh Ahura Mazda, I beg of you, grant to Frashaoshtra the most pleasing refuge found in Asha, and to me that which virtuous Xshatra, who is of you, will grant. Let us be dear to one another for all eternity!

49.9: Let that helper, charitable as is their nature, listen to the teachings. That one who speaks simply does not support wherever those aligned to Druj find refuge. Oh Jamaspa, bind their spiritual knowledge to Asha so that they may be bound as well to the most magnificent of treasures as shall be promised to them.

49.10: Oh Mazda, this is what you store in your palace: The

virtuous thoughts, the souls of the Ashavans, and the praise and animal fat we provide to you so that Armaiti may be abundant through Xshatra.

49.11: However, those aligned to Druj, who are unenlightened tyrants who act and speak unvirtuously, and who hold unvirtuous spiritual views, will have their souls bring them the rotten foods, as is due to them as welcome guests in the palace of Druj.

49.12: What help can you, through Asha, provide for me, Zarathushtra, who calls for it? What do you provide through Vohu Manah? Oh Ahura Mazda, I will be ever devoted and praise you, pleading that, as you authorize, you grant me the most magnificent things.

Yasna 50

50.1: Does my soul deserve aid? Oh Ahura Mazda, the defender of the cattle, who is not Asha or you, has been found so be quick and bring me enlightenment.

50.2: Oh Mazda, how does one even convince those cattle that bring us so much joy? They wish for one to belong to, to provide them with fields, one who lives an honest life with Asha even if they live around those who prefer to never see the sun. I, who should be accepted as just, will be the one who will sit with them.

50.3: Oh Mazda, it is through Asha that they will belong to him, as he has been assigned what is of Xshatra through Vohu Manah. He may make fruitful, through the strength of his gifts, the nearest herd, which the Drujvan will surrender to him.

50.4: Oh Ahura Mazda, I, who am enlightened, will worship and praise you and Asha, and, with Xshatra alongside me, I can now follow that path which strengthens me even when faced with those who are spirited, and where my request to be heard and welcomed in your palace is not ignored.

50.5: Oh Ahura, you have made it so, you who through Asha are the wisest of them all, as you are pleased with your Manthran and have made manifest and clear your aid, sent by you who brings us the comfort of your embrace.

50.6: Oh Mazda, that resounding manthra comes from the voice of Zarathushtra, he, who through Asha and in reverence, is your ally. May the bestower of enlightenment thus enlighten me further so that my very words serve as the charioteers of my prayers.

50.7: I will bind the swiftest steeds to bring you praises, and their victories shall be extensive, and strong through Vohu Manah. Oh Mazda, it is through Asha that you will send them forward so that you may provide me with aid.

50.8: Oh Mazda, with very many footsteps, I will attend to you as I have proclaimed, with my hands outstretched, with reverence towards you, who are ever spirited and full of Asha, who are the master of enlightenment.

50.9: Oh Mazda, with such worship and praise I will approach you again, with enlightened deeds done through Asha, when I will have the authority to receive what was promised to me when I wish it. May I then be full of strength through such charitable grace.

50.10: Oh Ahura Mazda, I will perform those deeds presently, which will be found worthy through the sight of Vohu Manah, in the light of the sun and in the presence of the rising bull of the day, that which is your praise done through Asha.

50.11: Oh Mazda, I have declared myself the one who praises you and thus I will be, as much as I am able, and as Asha grants me the authority to be. The one who provides what is will expand, through enlightenment, the manifestation of the most magnificent ideas.

The Vohuxshatra Gatha

Yasna 51

51.1: We welcome Xshatra, who amazes us with blessings and bounties, he who gives freely of his riches, and transfers them to us through Asha. Oh Mazda, I will, through my deeds, provide only the most magnificent for us.

51.2: Oh Ahura Mazda, thus will I first display the strength that Xshatra has provided, to you and to Asha, and to you, Armaiti. Through Vohu Manah, may you grant us your praiseworthy blessings.

51.3: Be that Ahura, who through Asha, focuses your listening on those who find refuge in your deeds. Oh Mazda, do this through your enlightened declarations, which through your words you remain that master who was before what is

51.4: When the joy of patronage comes, where will it come full of compassion? Where is Asha honored? What about that bountiful Armaiti? Where is enlightenment to be found? Oh Mazda, where, through Xshatra, who is of you, is this place?

51.5: The questions remain about the many ways in which, through Asha, the cow may be found by the herder, whose deeds are highly esteemed and is enlightened through reverence, and who through the authority that belongs to Ashi, provides a fair assessment of the just.

51.6: They who decide to align themselves to what is beyond magnificence and heed his will shall be the ones who the Ahura, through Xshatra, will remember. Alas, those that do not care for him are terribly cursed if they remain this way even at the final renovation of what is.

51.7: Oh Mazda, who fashioned the cow, the plants, and the Apas, may Ameretat and Haurvatat be with me through your most bountiful spirit, along with the might and vigor declared by Vohu Manah.

51.8: Oh Mazda, I will tell you, though you may already know, that what the Drujvan sees as cursed is what one who embraces Asha truly desires. Most happy is the devotee who speaks to one who is so knowing.

51.9: Oh Mazda, you are pleased to dispense harmony through crimson Atar, and even in molten metal are these vital forces seen without issue. When you bless the Ashavan, the Drujvan weakens.

51.10: Oh Mazda, he who constantly attempts to destroy me, that spawn of the source of Druj, is obviously uncharitable to all. I call for Asha and Ashi to join me now!

51.11: Oh Mazda, who is it that is the ally of Zarathushtra Spitama? Who learned of the wisdom of Asha? Of bountiful Armaiti? Which of the eminences recognized enlightenment when it was offered?

51.12: It was not the beloved slave of that Kavi who, at the coming of winter, displeased Zarathushtra Spitama when he arrived as a messenger and was left at the door, and in the cold, with these two "gifts" being considered hospitality.

51.13: It is true, then, that the spiritual views of the Drujvan ignore what is obvious. Their soul, when shown that they wandered off the path of Asha through their own deeds and words, will shudder at the Chinvat Bridge.

51.14: The Karapans, who are found in the fields, are not supporters of your authority, who through their own deeds and declarations show that they are scornful of the cows that have been provided through patronage. It is their declarations that will finally bring them towards the palace of Druj.

51.15: Ahura Mazda, who was before what is, welcomes those sacrificers into his palace as Zarathushtra has promised

them. They have declared themselves to you, Vohu
Manah, and to Asha, ready for their blessings.

51.16: It is through his authority that Kavi Vishtaspa provides
these offerings on his journeys to seek enlightenment, so
that he may perceive what the bountiful Ahura Mazda has
realized through Asha. Let what is sought be revealed.

51.17: Frashaoshtra Hvogva has sworn his body, which I cherish,
to the virtuous spiritual teachings. May Ahura Mazda,
through his authority, make him strong, so that he may
find the grace of Asha.

51.18: Jamaspa Hvogva seeks the glory of enlightenment, which
he has chosen through Asha, and Xvarenah who was
chosen to be bestowed by Xshatra. Oh Ahura Mazda, my
advocate, grant me all that you can.

51.19: Oh, it is he, and Maidyoimaongha Spitama, that have
chosen for themselves to accept the spiritual teachings,
and, who in attempting to secure what is, recite those
declarations of Mazda which make mortal deeds more
virtuous.

51.20: So that all of you harmonious ones may grant us the
blessings which Asha and Vohu Manah provide, we
worship with reverence, and with the declarations from
Armaiti, Mazda our constant advocate.

51.21: It is through unity with Armaiti, with the enlightened
deeds thus declared, that this blessed one causes Asha
to prosper through the spiritual teachings. Ahura Mazda
grants enlightenment through Xshatra and I plead with
him for the blessings of Ashi.

51.22: Ahura Mazda knows who aligns themselves to Asha so
that they may provide worthy worship. I will worship
those, with my brethren, who are and have been before
what is, and I will provide for them with love.

The Vahishtoishti Gatha

Yasna 53

53.1: Zarathushtra Spitama will be known for his magnificent abilities, since Ahura Mazda has granted to him, and all those who practice and master the declarations and deeds of the spiritual teachings, a blessed and virtuous life for eternity.

53.2: Let them then, enlightened as they are, join devotedly in the acknowledgement and praise and worship of Mazda through their declarations and deeds, joined by Kavi Vishtaspa, and the son of Zarathushtra Spitama, and Frashaoshtra, who have the ordained paths before them, which are the treasures which were established by the Ahura through the spiritual teachings of the Saoshyants.

53.3: Oh Pourucista, you who come from the line of Haecataspa Spitama, the youngest of all the daughters of Zarathushtra, it is through your devotion to the enlightenment that Asha and Mazda provide that you have found such a refuge. Thus, by the aid of your enlightened mind, will you find this refuge with one most bountiful and charitable as is praised by Armaiti.

53.4: You will care for him as you have cared for your father, and the herdsmen, and the family: With your enveloping eagerness, for you are a woman of Asha among those who align to Asha. Ahura Mazda grants the bright harvest of enlightenment to you, who values her bonds with her kin, and to the virtuous spiritual teachings for eternity.

53.5: All of you girls about to be married and you as well, listen to the lessons I share. Remember and accept them as you have the spiritual teachings, for these are in accord with them, and with the enlightened life. Let each of you seek to surpass the other in Asha as this will be beneficial for you and him.

53.6: Oh, you men and women, this is in all respects the truth. If you witness one rely on Druj in their motives, know that I will render them defenseless, and Vayu will deprive of comfort those who offer that rotten food that comes from the tyrants who align to Druj and oppress those of Asha. If you side with them, you destroy your own minds.

53.7: There will blessings for you, who are most pious, in this ritual of procreation, that will banish the Drujvan. For without this ritual, we would be most sorrowful in our speech.

53.8: Let those who are unvirtuous, wailing as they are prone to do, be shattered and exhausted by them. Let the virtuous rulers, who are surrounded by murderers and brutalizers, establish peace alongside them and all the settled clans, and let the greatly accursed ones, who shackle themselves to death, poison themselves as they do now.

53.9: Their poison spreads through their unwise decisions. They, who hide in darkness, abandon themselves through their greed and offense towards Asha. Where is the Ashavan Ahura that will see the freedoms and lives they have been given be declared bankrupt? Oh Mazda, it is through Xshatra that you grant what is greatest to the decent and the destitute.

The Holy Manthra: The Airyema-Ishyo

Yasna 54

54.1: May Airyaman bring aid to all people of Zarathushtra, and uphold the enlightened spiritual teachings, which deserve enviable praise. I plead for the empowerment, which Ashi provides through Asha, as Ahura Mazda has ordained. (x4) Asha is virtuous and magnificent, and joy upon joy is what Asha provides, for thus is Asha Vahishta. (x3)

54.2: *We sacrifice the Airyema-Ishyo, which is mighty through Verethragna, who opposes all malevolent attacks, the most magnificent of the declarations provided to us through Asha. We also sacrifice to the bountiful Gathas which are the most supreme and holy section of the ritual. We also sacrifice to and praise the Yasna which were brought down to us from time immemorial.* They that are, who are of any gender, Ahura Mazda knows through Asha of their glorious sacrifices: Thus, we offer them worship!

Author Biography

Zarathushtra Spitama, believed to have lived somewhere between 2500–1000 BCE in Central Asia, is the founder of the ancient spiritual tradition known as Mazdayasna or, as it's popularly known in the English-speaking world, Zoroastrianism. He retells some of his life story in the Gathas, his own oral composition passed down through centuries in this fashion that was finally written down in the Sassanian Era. These ancient poems and the development of Mazdayasna was done by the instigation of Ahura Mazda, the highest divinity in the tradition that he developed. His legacy has outgrown Mazdayasna and Zarathushtra has been credited, evidenced and not, with the founding, development, and/or heavy influence of philosophy, astronomy, astrology, magic, ethics, political science, and much more. Even thousands of years later, Zarathushtra's name is still spoken worldwide, and he is considered one of the most important figures to have ever lived.

About the Translator

Pablo Vazquez, born in Panama and now living in Texas, is a scholar, author, translator, game writer, lecturer, and essayist. Currently working on their second graduate degree, an MDiv at Starr King in the USA, Pablo's first graduate degree was a MA in Religions of Asia and Africa from SOAS University of London where their concentration was in Zoroastrianism, Kurdish Studies, and New Religious Movements. While there, they were affiliated with the Shapoorji Pallonji Institute of Zoroastrian Studies where they learned Zoroastrian history, theology, and the Avestan language among other topics from some of the top scholars in the field. Pablo is also unique as an officially accepted convert into Zoroastrianism, having undergone their Sedreh Pooshi in 2018 in the United States, and having been invited to speak at Zoroastrian conferences and events. They are an active independent lecturer, having delivered lectures on a variety of spiritual, academic, and special interest topics in multiple countries. Pablo's hobbies include travel and pilgrimage, antiquarian artifacts and book collecting, tabletop roleplaying games, spirituality and mysticism, and trying out all sorts of delicious-looking dishes.

Note to Readers

Thank you for purchasing this book. My hope is that you derived as much from reading this book as I have in translating it. If you have a few moments, please feel free to add your review of the book at your favorite online site for feedback and to let any of your interested friends and colleagues know about it. It will help others also gain the wisdom of these texts which is my main goal. A portion of my royalties go towards Mazdayasni charities and organizations. Also, if you would like to learn more about Mazdayasna, arrange a lecture/interview with me, and/or be notified of other books on related topics that I have coming in the near future, please visit this website: https://www.mazdayasni.com.

Sincerely and with blessings,

P.V.

MANTRA
BOOKS

EASTERN RELIGION & PHILOSOPHY

We publish books on Eastern religions and philosophies. Books
that aim to inform and explore the various traditions that began in
the East and have migrated West.
If you have enjoyed this book, why not tell other readers by
posting a review on your preferred book site.

Recent bestsellers from MANTRA BOOKS are:

The Way Things Are
A Living Approach to Buddhism
Lama Ole Nydahl
An introduction to the teachings of the Buddha, and how to make use of these teachings in everyday life.
Paperback: 978-1-84694-042-2 ebook: 978-1-78099-845-9

Back to the Truth
5000 Years of Advaita
Dennis Waite
A demystifying guide to Advaita for both those new to, and those familiar with this ancient, non-dualist philosophy from India.
Paperback: 978-1-90504-761-1 ebook: 978-184694-624-0

Shinto: A celebration of Life
Aidan Rankin
Introducing a gentle but powerful spiritual pathway reconnecting humanity with Great Nature and affirming all aspects of life.
Paperback: 978-1-84694-438-3 ebook: 978-1-84694-738-4

In the Light of Meditation
Mike George
A comprehensive introduction to the practice of meditation and the spiritual principles behind it. A 10 lesson meditation programme with CD and internet support.
Paperback: 978-1-90381-661-5

A Path of Joy
Popping into Freedom
Paramananda Ishaya
A simple and joyful path to spiritual enlightenment.
Paperback: 978-1-78279-323-6 ebook: 978-1-78279-322-9

The Less Dust the More Trust
Participating in The Shamatha Project, Meditation and Science
Adeline van Waning, MD PhD
The inside-story of a woman participating in frontline meditation
research, exploring the interfaces of mind-practice, science and
psychology.
Paperback: 978-1-78099-948-7 ebook: 978-1-78279-657-2

I Know How To Live, I Know How To Die
The Teachings of Dadi Janki: A warm, radical, and life-affirming
view of who we are, where we come from, and what time is calling
us to do
Neville Hodgkinson
Life and death are explored in the context of frontier science and
deep soul awareness.
Paperback: 978-1-78535-013-9 ebook: 978-1-78535-014-6

Living Jainism
An Ethical Science
Aidan Rankin, Kanti V. Mardia
A radical new perspective on science rooted in intuitive awareness
and deductive reasoning.
Paperback: 978-1-78099-912-8 ebook: 978-1-78099-911-1

Ordinary Women, Extraordinary Wisdom
The Feminine Face of Awakening
Rita Marie Robinson
A collection of intimate conversations with female spiritual
teachers who live like ordinary women, but are engaged with their
true natures.
Paperback: 978-1-84694-068-2 ebook: 978-1-78099-908-1

The Way of Nothing
Nothing in the Way
Paramananda Ishaya
A fresh and light-hearted exploration of the amazing reality of
nothingness.
Paperback: 978-1-78279-307-6 ebook: 978-1-78099-840-4

Readers of ebooks can buy or view any of these bestsellers by
clicking on the live link in the title. Most titles are published in
paperback and as an ebook. Paperbacks are available in traditional
bookshops. Both print and ebook formats are available online.

Find more titles and sign up to our readers' newsletter at
http://www.johnhuntpublishing.com/mind-body-spirit.
Follow us on Facebook at https://www.facebook.com/OBooks
and Twitter at https://twitter.com/obooks.